IMAGES
of Sport

SHEFFIELD EAGLES

'EAGLES'
LIVE ON

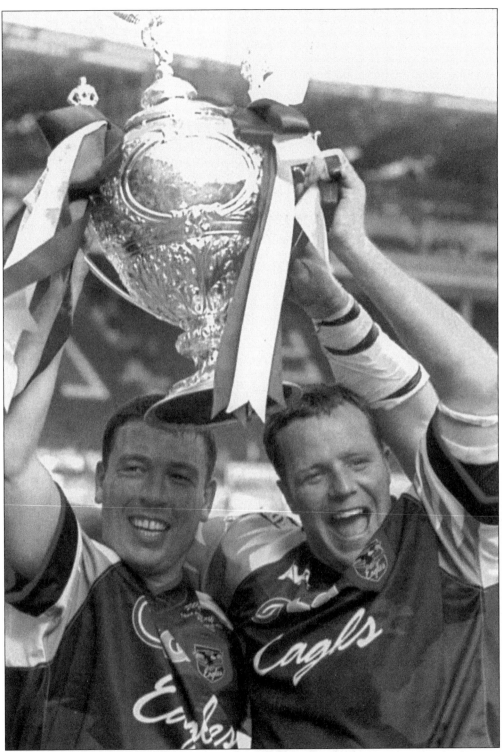

Mark Aston and Paul Broadbent hoist the Rugby League Challenge Cup after the historic victory over Wigan in the 1998 Cup Final.

IMAGES
of Sport

SHEFFIELD EAGLES

Compiled by
J.C. Cornwell

TEMPUS

First published 1999
Copyright © J.C. Cornwell, 1999

Tempus Publishing Limited
The Mill, Brimscombe Port,
Stroud, Gloucestershire, GL5 2QG

ISBN 0 7524 1830 0

Typesetting and origination by
Tempus Publishing Limited
Printed in Great Britain by
Midway Clark Printing, Wiltshire

*Front Cover: Eagles players celebrate on the pitch at Wembley after winning the
Rugby League Challenge Cup on 2 May 1998.*

Eagles players celebrate winning promotion to Division One after beating Chorley at Owlerton
on 2 April 1989.

Contents

A disconsolate Eagles mascot is sidelined after knee surgery in 1998. However, Freddy the Eagle carried on with his 'duties' despite needing a pair of crutches to see him through.

Acknowledgements

I would like to thank Laura Drabble of Sheffield Eagles, who willingly gave her time to type up the original draft of the captions and also several subsequent amended and corrected versions. Without her help over three months in the summer of 1999 this project would never have been completed.

I am especially grateful to Ralph Rimmer, the Eagles' chief executive, and Mike Turner, the former marketing manager, for their encouragement whilst writing the book and specifically for enabling me to have access to the club's photographic archives. Many of these archive photographs were taken for the club by Steve Braithwaite and Glenn Ashley and the majority of the images I have used are by them.

Richard Pepper, who co-operated with me on an earlier history of the Eagles' first decade, once again gave me tremendous help, checking the drafts for factual errors, making available a complete collection of matchday programmes for the home games in the 1990s and patiently answering my numerous queries for obscure pieces of information.

The programmes for the first ever season in 1984/85 were loaned to me by Stuart Sheard and I have used two or three of them in the book.

A special word of thanks to Graham Clay and Vicky Matthers of *League Express* who generously allowed me to use their photographs of the Eagles 1998 Rugby League Challenge Cup final victory and also to Andrew Varley, Paul Wickson, Tony and Joan Roberts and Angela and Chris Fowler for allowing me to use one or two key photographs they had taken. The cartoon by Ralph Whitworth appears by kind permission of Sheffield Newspapers.

Finally, particular thanks must go the Peter Charlton, the editor of the *Sheffield Star*, for making available the photographs of the early years of the Eagles that they hold on file. They were virtually the only resource available to me to illustrate the 1980s period of the club's history.

J.C. Cornwell

Introduction

Unlike most of the professional Rugby League clubs who can trace their origin back to the 'Great Schism' of 1895, or at least back to the early days of the twentieth century, Sheffield Eagles are a club of very recent origin.

Founded in 1984 they appeared to be just another of the hopeful expansion teams like Kent/Southend Invicta, Cardiff Blue Dragons/Bridgend, Fulham and (later) Scarborough Pirates, trying to establish the game in territory new to Rugby League.

It was the vision and determination of Gary and Kath Hetherington that created, nurtured and sustained the nascent club in South Yorkshire, only thirty miles from the game's West Riding heartland, but alien and indifferent territory none the less.

They deliberately selected Sheffield to start their new venture because it was a city of over a million people, with a considerable sporting tradition and a larger industrial and commercial base than almost any other city or town with a Rugby League team.

It was the Hetherington's intention to enter the Second Division in the 1983/84 season and a major sponsor was in place. Furthermore, they believed they had a deal to share Sheffield United's Bramall Lane ground. However, United cancelled this option and so Eagles' application went back a year until 2 September 1984 when they played their first ever League game and beat Rochdale Hornets 29-10 at Owlerton Stadium, their home for the next five years. Meanwhile, a second major set-back had seen the collapse of their sponsor's business, but Gary and Kath (now the first ever female member of the Rugby League Council) pressed ahead with the new season, although by December the club was within a whisker of folding because of their precarious financial position.

Necessity created a pattern for the club of carefully developing from the ground upwards, whilst making continual, seemingly inevitable, progress and at the same time keeping close contact with their supporters. It was important to establish a real sense of a community of enthusiasts struggling for recognition in an area where association football dominated the winter sporting scene.

However, progress was slow, the team finishing seventeenth in the first season and twelfth in 1985/86. They began to soar in the 1986/87 season with 17 wins, finishing sixth, and then went one better to fifth in 1987/88. In their fifth season they grabbed the third promotion spot and then celebrated success by winning the Second Division Premiership title at Old Trafford, beating much fancied Swinton by 43-18 points, Powell scoring a hat-trick.

That Premiership win made the Rugby League world take notice, but most pundits assumed that they would very quickly take the drop back to Division Two. A massive blow was struck to their ambitions when, following the Hillsborough tragedy, their Owlerton ground was declared closed to Rugby League. There followed the most amazing odyssey that would have broken the spirit of most clubs. Home matches were played on seven different grounds, including Hillsborough and Bramall Lane – where on 8 October 1989 Eagles came of age when they outplayed Widnes, the new World Club Champions, and won 31-6. They just survived that first season, but the second season in the top division saw them relegated, but not before they had beaten St Helens and Widnes, drawn with Wigan and completely humiliated Hull KR by 62-16 points.

A quick return was forecast for Eagles in the new eight team Second Division and they did not disappoint. They won the League and won the Premiership with another glorious day at Old Trafford, this time over Oldham, thereby climbing back into Division One where they remained throughout the 1990s.

After 1992 the Eagles established themselves as a First Division side and latterly became one of the founding members of Super League in 1996. Between these two dates they restored the old sense of inevitable progress, a big city club who finally achieved victories over all the top teams, including a first win over Wigan at the Don Valley in 1994. They also reached the final of the Yorkshire Cup in 1993, put four tries past the Australian 1993 World Cup squad, considered a merger with Doncaster RLFC and participated in the end of the season First Division Premiership play-offs.

They even tried an Australian coach for half a season in 1993 before Gary Hetherington took back the reins and continued to guide the club, on and off the field, until his shock departure at the end of 1996. Meanwhile, Eagles had enthusiastically enhanced the new Super League concept and had been selected to play in the new competition's opening fixture in Paris in March 1996. Despite losing that match they finished the 1996 season in a respectable seventh place, leaving them poised to become one of Rugby League's leading sides. It came as a bombshell to players, officials and fans alike when the club's founder, Gary Hetherington, unexpectedly left Sheffield to run Leeds RLFC. However, new people took over the management with Phil Larder having a brief interlude as coach before the team settled down under John Kear's leadership.

There was a new owner, the club became the first Rugby League club to be floated on the Stock Exchange and by the end of the 1997 season they once again reached the Premiership play-off semi-finals. Even more dramatically they had recorded the first home British win over an Australian club, the Perth Reds, in the 1997 World Club Challenge, a competition in which British teams did spectacularly badly on the whole.

To those who had long supported the Eagles and the directors and staff who had nurtured their development, it always appeared that this progress was leading to some great consummation, some major triumph that would finally reward all the years of missionary toil in South Yorkshire. It came in sensational fashion on 2 May 1998 when Eagles outplayed and defeated Wigan in the Rugby League Challenge Cup at Wembley, a result that left most of the sporting world in profound disbelief but absolute delight.

That victory summed up all that was true about the Eagles – self-confident, determined outsiders, well regarded by fans of neutral clubs whilst not fully appreciated in their home town. Even the City Council had not expected them to win and had to hastily convene a civic reception for the team who had brought back a prestigious national trophy to a city that demands achievement in sport. In the films, the credits would roll now, but in real life there is a continuum and the rest of the 1998 season and the subsequent 1999 fourth Super League season were more of a plateau than a further surge of achievement on the pitch.

At the end of the 1999 season, cataclysmic events off the pitch saw the merger of the club with the Huddersfield Giants and the end of the Eagles as an independent club solely based in the city of Sheffield. The rights and wrongs of this decision will not be fully understood until the dust settles, but clearly it was driven by financial pressures and the new merged club may go on to have a successful future.

However, in October there emerged a further proposal to create a new Sheffield Eagles as a First Division club and a possible return to the Owlerton Stadium. If this initiative gets off the ground, the club's history will have turned full circle since 1984. Whatever new developments take place, Eagles' fifteen year rise from obscurity cup winners will irrevocably remain a part of the folklore of Rugby League.

J.C. Cornwell
Sheffield, October 1999

One
The Fledgling
Club Takes Off
1984-87

The Eagles team that took the field in the first ever game against Rochdale Hornets on 2 September 1984 at Owlerton Stadium. From left to right, back row: Vince Farrar, Andy Tyers, Daryl Powell, Gary Hetherington, Ian Jowitt, Mark S. Campbell, Billy Harris, John Gregory, Mark Q. Campbell. Front row: Ray Smith, Steve Robinson, Steve Cooper, Paul Welsh, Paul McDermott, Dave Alred.

David Betts, the first chairman of the Eagles, in June 1984 with the winning entry to the competition to name the club organised through the *Sheffield Star*. Darren Porter of Chapman Street, Sheffield came up with the winning name at a time when most Rugby League clubs were just proudly called only by the name of their town. Eagles needed a suffix if they were to establish themselves in the land of Wednesday and United and later the Steelers and the Sharks.

In August 1984, just before the season started, the new kit was unveiled to supporters. Here, nineteen year old Sarah Rawlinson of Darton, who was working as a temporary club secretary prior to going to college, models the new strip. It had not been the product of great discussion over numerous alternative designs, but was one selected by the Huddersfield manufacturer and sent at almost the last minute. In 1984 it was quite a daring design but it would only last for one season; Eagles would go on to play in every colour in the rainbow over the next fifteen years.

The Eagles programme cover (right) and the Eagles and Rochdale Hornets line-ups (below) for that historic first game, which Eagles won 29-10. Gary Hetherington was keen that the new club entered the second division in some style and the programme was of considerably better design than most of its contemporaries in the lower division.

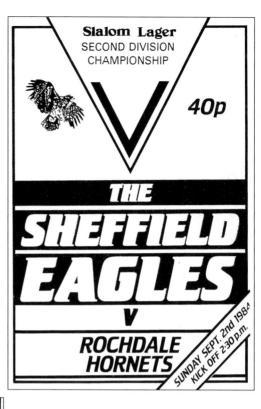

Slalom Lager
SECOND DIVISION CHAMPIONSHIP

40p

THE

SHEFFIELD EAGLES

v

ROCHDALE HORNETS

SUNDAY SEPT. 2nd 1984
KICK OFF 2.30 p.m.

SHEFFIELD EAGLES v ROCHDALE HORNETS

SHEFFIELD EAGLES Claret, Gold & White		ROCHDALE HORNETS Blue with Red & White trim
Andy TYERS	1 (Full Back)	Kevin SIMPKIN
Ray SMITH	2 (Right Wing)	Phil CARTWRIGHT
Daryl POWELL	3 (Right Centre)	Andy BARKER
Mark CAMPBELL	4 (Left Centre)	Steve FENNEY
Dave ALRED	5 (Left Wing)	Mark MASSA
Steve ROBINSON	6 (Stand Off)	Alan FAIRHURST
A.N. OTHER	7 (Scrum Half)	Brian HUGHES
Billy HARRIS	8 (Openside Prop)	Dave CHISNALL
Gary HETHERINGTON	9 (Hooker)	Kevin LOWE
Vince FARRAR	10 (Blindside Prop)	Martin GRATTAN
Steve COOPER	11 (2nd Row Forward)	Jim MOLYNEUX
Ian JOWITT	12 (2nd Row Forward)	Rod HASLAM
Paul McDERMOTT	13 (Loose Forward)	Billy PLATT
A.N. OTHER	14 (Substitute)	George CLAUGHTON
John GREGORY	15 (Substitute)	Terry LANGAN

SUBSTITUTES: Each Team is allowed two substitutes and the players in the original 13 who are replaced by substitutes can themselves act as a substitute, but only once.
SCORING: A try counts as four points. A penalty goal or a conversion counts as two points. A drop goal is one point.

MATCH OFFICIALS

Referee
Mr F. LINDOP (Wakefield)

Touch Judges
Mr D. WATSON   red flag
Mr T.J. BROWN   gold flag

Todays *mitre*
Matchball donated by

WORRALL NEWS
(Graham Crapper & Jim Dale)
Tel: Sheffield 348819

YOUR NEXT GAME SUNDAY 9th SEPTEMBER
SHEFFIELD EAGLES v FULHAM

Printed by "PRINTING PLUS" 205 Middlewood Road, Sheffield. S6 4HD Tel (0427) 334167
"PRINTING PLUS" is a trading name of Postmark Limited

The team sheet for Eagles contains a couple of A.N. Others – that stalwart Rugby League 'player' who often graced team sheets in past decades.

A youthful Gary Hetherington's first message to the fans contained in the match programme that day was 'Bringing Rugby League to Sheffield has been done in the belief that you, the supporter, will enjoy watching the game and encourage others to do so'. He added, somewhat prophetically, 'It is unlikely we will win the Challenge Cup this season but with your continual support we can go on and be a major force in the game'.

Vince Farrar is tackled by a Rochdale second row forward with Billy Harris in support and Gary Hetherington, playing hooker, observing his props in action.

Ray Smith, who came on as a sub after ten minutes, galvanised the team into action. Eagles, who had been 10-0 down, then scored six tries, including a Paul McDermott hat-trick, to gain a very satisfactory 29-10 victory. Here, Smith is being tackled whilst Paul Welsh backs up.

Kath Hetherington, on the left, with Barbara Close of Fulham after the second game, a 14-18 defeat against Fulham at Owlerton. Kath was a key figure in the development of the Eagles club from day one. She also was the first woman to be elected to the Rugby League Council. Although there were no regulations banning women from serving on the council, the majority of members disgracefully voted against her membership. However, they needed a two-thirds majority to ban Kath and they just failed to achieve this. Years later in 1995, the game's centenary year, she would be a high profile President of the RFL. Again, she was the first woman to achieve this honour.

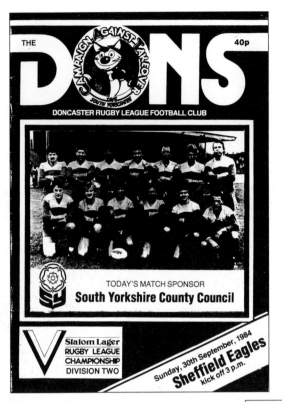

The first ever South Yorkshire Rugby League derby match was played at Tattersfield on 30 September 1984. Doncaster, who were emerging from a period of many years as one of Rugby Leagues' most unsuccessful teams, beat Eagles 18-10. The game was sponsored by the old South Yorkshire County Council, who, like the GLC and the other Metropolitan Counties, were under sentence of death after Margaret Thatcher's 1983 election victory.

The programme for the Bridgend Blue Dragons game in February 1985 may have been basic, but the game itself was possibly the lowest point in the Eagles' playing history. The Blue Dragons had moved from Cardiff after an unsuccessful 1983/84 season. They only survived one more season in professional Rugby League and only won one game that season. Eagles were the victims going down 28-12 to the Welsh side, who shortly afterwards went out of business. Gary Hetherington was so ashamed of his team that he wrote a letter of apology to all the travelling supporters. (Not a vast army, as only twenty-three attended). The Eagles eventually finished seventeenth in the League in their first season with 8 wins out of 28 games played.

BLUE DRAGONS

welcomes

SHEFFIELD R.L.F.C.

COYCHURCH ROAD, BRIDGEND.

2 4 FEB 1985   Kick Off: 3·00 p.m.

Official Match Magazine 30p

Eagles started the second season in a more confident mood with some new signings, including the first Australians: Scott Wright, Mitchell Sherwood and Paul Kuhnemann. The 1985/86 squad was, from left to right, back row: Gamson, Wright, Farrell, Bridgeman, Glancy, Campbell. Middle row: Alan Rhodes (coach), Sherwood, Harris, Kuhnemann, Rafferty, Redfern, Brook (assistant coach). Front row: Tomlinson (physiotherapist), Welsh, Lane (captain), Powell, Wileman.

Eagles brought out a new maroon strip for the second season. Largely modelled on the Washington Redskins uniform, it had a new badge that looked uncommonly like that of Manly Sea Eagles. Here Julie Bush, the long-serving club secretary, models the strip whilst sat precariously on Gary Hetherington's shoulders. Steve Lane makes up the trio.

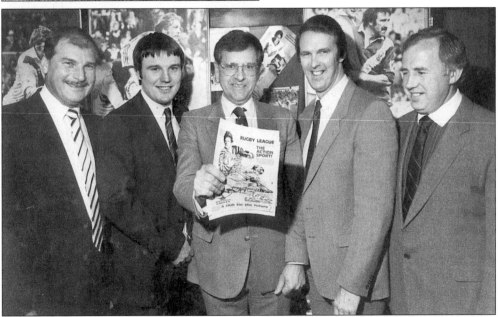

Board members Gerry Mullins, Terry Sharman and Mel Bedford join Gary Hetherington and the Rugby Football League's PRO, David Howes, to launch Eagles' new season. The board had had a desperate time in the first season keeping their heads above the financial waters. However, they were in optimistic mood as they proclaimed Eagles as being 'A club for the future'. They were right, as for every season until 1991 the club made significant advances each year.

Steve Ferres joined the club in 1986 and played five games before settling down to a seven year period as the assistant coach. His partnership with Gary Hetherington was to gain Eagles the Second Division Premiership twice, as well as promotion to Division One in 1989 and 1992. He later went on to successfully coach Hunslet and take Huddersfield into Super League. He is now chief executive at Wakefield Trinity.

Gary Hetherington landed a major sponsor in Whitbread plc. Initially, the deal was to run for two years but it lasted over a decade. Gary was given ten minutes to state his case to this giant brewery and leisure company but he so convinced them of Eagles' future prospects that a successful and very happy partnership was established. Daryl Powell, soon to be the captain of the club, and Gary Hetherington are pictured here receiving the first sponsorship cheque. Chris Morrin of Whitbread spots the ball.

New Zealanders Mark Roiall (left) and Paddy Burgoyne work out at a Sheffield health club. Eagles were to be well served by Kiwi players and Sam Panapa, who would return for a second spell in the 1990/91 season, was amongst the first players from the 'Land of the long white cloud'.

The 1986/87 season saw Eagles rise to a creditable sixth position. They clearly were now an established team with serious ambitions to gain promotion to the top division. The team who turned out for the 22-20 win over Doncaster in the Yorkshire Cup in September was, from left to right, back row: Hetherington (coach/manager), Harris, Lidbury, Bridgeman, Kuhnemann, Miller, Rafferty, Glancy, Farrell, Sherwood, Dr David Durie (director). Front row: Smith, Cholmondley, Lane, Gamson, Powell, Dickinson.

Eagles were succeeding well enough to be named the Team of the Month for September 1986, for which they received the princely sum of £250. Steve Lane, the captain, for whom this would be the last season with the Eagles, receives the framed certificate and the cheque. Eagles had earned the award by winning all four League games and a Yorkshire Cup round against Doncaster under their new coach Gary Hetherington.

Derek Bridgeman in action against Mansfield Marksman in the first game of the season. Derek was an immensely popular forward who had originally been signed in 1984 as a winger. In five seasons until 1989 he played in 119 games, scoring 25 tries, despite having a serious arm disability which would have stopped lesser men from ever starting a Rugby League career.

Mark Gamson, Eagles' second signing in 1984, is awarded the Man of the Match award against Hunslet, a game Eagles won 16-12 in March 1987. Signed from Leeds Colts, Mark was another of the Eagles fans' great favourites, primarily for his sheer guts and determination. He played 343 games for the club, in almost every position on the team sheet, between 1984 and 1997 and still holds the club record for first team appearances.

In March 1987 the Sheffield and District Amateur Rugby League Development Association (SADARLDA) was formed at a Civic Reception in Sheffield Town Hall. Over the last twelve years it has carried the Rugby League gospel into most of the primary and secondary schools in Sheffield and also in Rotherham and Barnsley. Eagles have always supported SADARLDA and many of their top players over the years have taken a regular part in school and club coaching. Joining the Lord Mayor, Councillor Frank Prince, at the opening was, from left to right: Maurice Oldroyd (BARLA), John Cornwell (SADARLDA), Gary Hetherington, the Lord Mayor, Councillor Peter Price (Sheffield) and Councillor Joe Allott (Rotherham).

Two
On the Road
to Promotion
1987-89

Gary Hetherington, who predicted it would take the Eagles five years to reach the top division, celebrates with his mud-soaked team after they had beaten Chorley 26-6 at Owlerton on 2 April 1989 and clinched promotion. Ten years on only Mark Aston (at the rear to the left of the champagne bottle) was still with the club.

Neil Kellet, a very popular prop forward, tries his hand behind the camera during a team photographic session before the start of the 1987/88 season. He had signed for the Eagles the previous season from Mansfield Marksman in a pub car park on his way to a match at Hunslet. He played 73 games between then and 1991, scoring 19 tries for the club.

Another day of glorious mud at Tattersfield as Eagles beat the Dons 32-2 just after Christmas in December 1987. Ironically, they chose their rarely used all-white shirts and only Paul McDermott is clearly identifiable as he watches the tackle. A substantial area in front of the Tattersfield 25 used to flood on the days like this and teams had to plan their tactics around it. It was weather like this that encouraged forward thinkers to campaign for summer Rugby League.

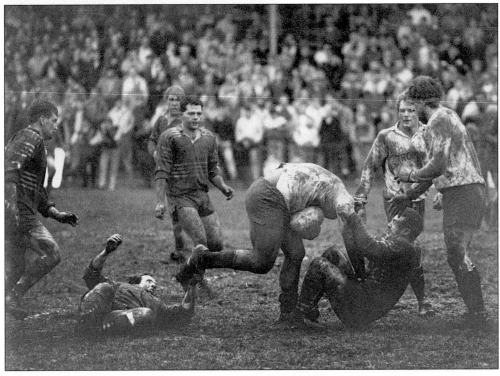

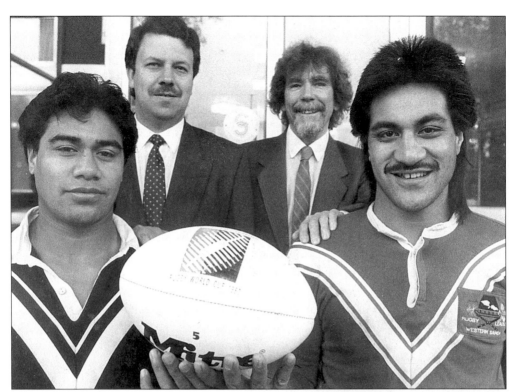

Bill Michie MP (on the right at the rear) poses with Kiwis Paul Okesene and 'Tiny' Solomona. Also in the picture is George Cohen, manager of the Hallam Tower Hotel where the players stayed. It had proved difficult to get the New Zealanders work permits, but the MP for Sheffield Heeley, found a way through the impasse and they signed for the club in October 1988.

Steve Evans was another signing in the promotional year. He was something of a coup for the Sheffield side, having recently been a Great Britain international and in the early eighties had been regarded as one of the big future stars of the British game. Signed from Hull FC he added a touch of class to the Eagles' backs and scored 9 tries in his 30 games for the club.

Left: Mark Geyer bemoans the theft of his boots on arriving in England in November 1988. Already considered a future Australian test prospect, the Penrith Panthers forward added some real punch to the Eagles pack for the brief six-match visit he made to the UK. He later went on to gain international honours for the Kangaroos and enjoyed a controversial career down under. Ironically, he would have returned to Sheffield with the Perth Western Reds in July 1997, but was suspended at the time. His younger brother Matt did play in a game that was one of Eagles' all-time great victories.

Below: Paul Okesene brings the ball up in the Rugby League Cup second round tie in February 1989 against Oldham. Having beaten Leigh, a team they were repeatedly drawn to play in the Rugby League Cup, by 23-17 points they went out 32-20 to their First Division opponents at Owlerton.

Eagles 'chair' their tailor, Ashley Rogers of Manor Top, who provided the squad with smart blazers. Howard Cartwright, third from right, was the Eagles' assistant coach who had played for Castleford and coached Lock Lane ARLFC. One of his proteges there was the young Paul Broadbent, who Howard introduced to the club. In 1993 he would leave Eagles and join Garry Jack as part of the Salford coaching team.

'Tiny' Solomona, later a Kiwi international in the 1993 New Zealand tour of Great Britain, was voted Man of the Match against Leigh in a 30-17 defeat at Owlerton in October 1988. Leigh were one of the four strongest teams in the Second Division that season and Eagles also lost at Hilton Park before winning in the Challenge Cup. The sponsors on the day were Sheffield Co-op, who were regular supporters of the Eagles for most of this season. Harold Schofield (centre) and Harry Twigg (right) present 'Tiny' with his brandy and decanter set. He played only 5 games for the Eagles in 1988 before returning home after a family bereavement.

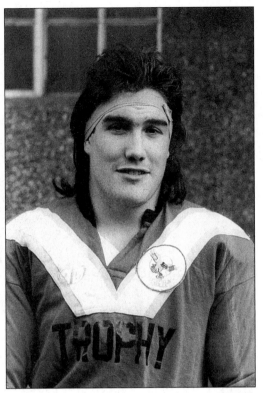

Nick Grimoldby signed for the club in January 1989 and made his debut in a fine 42-4 win at Batley, also scoring one of the tries. Eagles at that stage had won five consecutive games and were beginning to look serious contenders for one of the three promotional spots. Nick would remain at Sheffield until 1994, playing 70 games and scoring 11 tries. Later he would become the chairman of the Rugby League Players Union, a position once held by Gary Hetherington.

Nick Halafihi was another signing in 1988 who strengthened the depth of the Eagles squad. He joined the club as a centre from Carnegie College, where he had played in student Rugby League. Born in the East Riding, his Tongan father Nan had played in the centre for Hull FC in the 1960 Cup Final. In the opening match of the season, Nick scored in the win over Bramley and in the following season he would play against Widnes at Bramall Lane in one of Eagles' greatest victories. He left to go to London Crusaders and later, in 1999, he became the Rugby Football League's director of development.

The side that eventually won promotion pictured at Owlerton in late 1988. From left to right, back row: Clive Hindle (kit man), Wilders, P. Cartwright, Hetherington, Idle, Okesene, Geyer, Evans, Broadbent, Young, Halafihi, Ward, Kellett, Cunningham (dentist), C. McDermott. Front row: Nelson, Gamson, Dickinson, Powell, Aston, Cook, P. McDermott, Close, H. Cartwright, Dr Durie, Ferres.

Gary Van Bellen also made his debut for the Eagles in January 1989. A player with considerable first-class experience he was to give the pack extra power. He had come on a free transfer but gained a new lease of life at Sheffield. He played a significant part in the Premiership win at Old Trafford in May and remained with Eagles until the end of the 1989/90 season.

David Close hoists the champagne bottle as Eagles celebrate gaining promotion after defeating Chorley 26-8 at Owlerton. In an undistinguished game played in atrocious conditions the Eagles gained the third promotion place behind Leigh and Barrow. On the front row of this famous picture are Andy Young, David Close, Paul Broadbent, Mark Gamson, Warren Smiles and Sonny Nickle.

Nick Grimoldby comes off the pitch after the Chorley game – the joy of winning promotion superseding the exhaustion of a game played in thick mud and driving rain.

One month later at Old Trafford Eagles defeated Swinton in the Second Division Premiership final by the overwhelming margin of 43-18 points. Daryl Powell, already in the Great Britain training squad, got a hat-trick on the day and holds the trophy high as Mark Aston and Paul Broadbent join in the cheers.

The Lord Mayor, Councillor Tony Damms, hosts a reception for Eagles' promotion and Premiership winning side at Sheffield Town Hall. The line-up is, from left to right: Mark Aston, Warren Smiles, Phil Cartwright, Paul Broadbent, Daryl Powell, Andy Young, Gary Hetherington, The Lord Mayor, Dr David Durie, Peter Wilders and Terry Sharman.

Warren Smiles and his wife Ros celebrate the dual success. They got married shortly after joining the Eagles and Ros worked in the front office. Warren, from Western Australia, had been released by Bramley and replaced Mark Geyer in the Eagles squad. For the next two seasons he would give many gritty performances for the club, scoring 5 tries in his 32 games before returning to Perth in 1990 to become a Rugby League development officer.

Ever mindful of the need to bring on new talent, Eagles ran an under-17s team in the late 1980s. In the background are the superb bar facilities at Owlerton stadium, which helped to encourage sponsors and fans. However, the 1988/89 season would be the last one at Owlerton because of new regulations in the aftermath of the Hillsborough disaster.

Three

Up, Down and Up Again
1989-92

Paul Broadbent scoring the Eagles' first ever try in the First Division against St Helens at Hillsborough on 3 September 1989. After leading for two-thirds of the game, St Helens' extra class proved too much and they eventually won 36-20. Because of the tragedy that had occurred at this ground during the FA Cup semi-final the previous April, new regulations had banned the use of Owlerton for Rugby League. Eagles would spend the season playing their home games at seven different grounds – not an easy welcome to the tough demands of the First Division.

Eagles fans pictured at Featherstone after they had walked twenty miles from Birdwell to the Rovers 'ground for Eagles' first away match in the First Division. This fundraising march raised £1,300 for the club, who were now attaining sizeable support for their games, both home and away. The march did the trick and Eagles beat 'Fev' to record their first win in the First Division.

David Mycoe, signed by Gary Hetherington on his seventeenth birthday. A promising cricketer, who might have gone on to play for Yorkshire, he had been playing with Crigglestone ARLFC and Hetherington signed him on his reputation, never having seen him play. He went straight into the first team for the game against St Helens at Hillsborough and was the youngest player in the First Division that season.

Anthony Farrell signs for Eagles in October 1989 from Huddersfield. Gary Hetherington and Neil Shuttleworth of the Fartown club shake hands on the deal whilst Farrell looks on. At £55,000 this was Eagles' record signing as Anthony was a promising centre, with three Great Britain under-21 and two Great Britain Colts caps to his credit. He would score 35 tries in 138 games for Eagles until the end of the 1996 season, when he was transferred to the Leeds Rhinos.

Eagles fans had to get on the bus to support their team home or away. Eagles played two games at Hillsborough and two at Bramall Lane that season, but also played home games at the grounds of soccer clubs Chesterfield FC and Barnsley FC. They played four games at Tattersfield, Doncaster RLFC's ground, and also one match each at Halifax's Thrum Hall and Wakefield Trinity's Belle Vue Ground.

Eagles players move in to defend in the Wigan game at Hillsborough in November 1989. The Eagles players, from left to right: Hardy, Aston and Dickinson. Jeff Hardy was an 'unknown' Australian from Illawarra who scored 13 tries in 20 games for Eagles that season. Almost ten years later he would return to the club for Super League IV.

Daryl Powell and Sonny Nickle dispose of a Hull player in the final game of the season at Bramall Lane. Although Eagles lost 32-4 to one of the strongest teams in Rugby League at that time, they had done enough to reach eleventh position in the league, with nine wins and a draw, and so avoided relegation

Eagles' plight is summed up in the Whitworth cartoon in the *Sheffield Telegraph*. Whitworth was a famous local cartoonist whose work was very familiar to people in South Yorkshire.

" Even the rugby team I support is homeless."

Don Valley Stadium became Eagles' home for the 1990/91 season. Built for the World Student Games due to be held a year later in July 1991. This meant that Eagles now had the most modern ground in Rugby League, with a 25,000 all-seater stadium, superb training and changing facilities and public toilets that a hotel would have been proud of!

David Mycoe undergoes a perfectly executed front on tackle. After two wins and a draw in their first three games, Eagles lost eight league and one cup game in succession and were struggling to keep out of the relegation zone by Christmas 1990.

Sonny Nickle breaks through the Warrington defence to score one of his two tries against the Wire at the Don Valley on 30 September 1990. Despite his performance, Eagles were narrowly beaten 18-20.

Hugh Waddell, the Scottish born prop, became a great favourite with the Eagles supporters for his determined running and hit-ups in attack. He joined Eagles at the end of the 1989/90 season, having already played six times for Great Britain, which included the great victory in the Third Test at Sydney in 1988 and the 1988 Hall of Fame match against the Rest of the World.

Encouraged by Eagles' success, a Sheffield Women's team had started in 1989, led by teachers Sue Jackson (third from left, front row) and Tracey Solman (extreme right, front row). They more than held their own in the WARLA Second Division. Later they would join Hillsborough Hawks ARLFC and develop a girls' team as well.

Richard Price joined the Eagles from Hull FC at the end of the 1990/91 season. In 166 appearances for the Sheffield club he scored 54 tries and was ever present in both the 1992/93 and the 1993/94 seasons (during which he was never substituted). A classy and elusive centre or stand-off, he holds the club record of 79 consecutive first team games.

Aston prepares to put the ball into the rear area of the scrum as Eagles go down narrowly to Castleford by 20-24 points at the Don Valley in March 1990. From left to right, awaiting the outcome of the scrum: Mycoe (under posts), Mumby, Price and Powell. Four consecutive close defeats in March sealed Eagles' relegation fears. They ended the season in thirteenth place, having won 7 and drawn 2 games. Only Rochdale Hornets were below them at the bottom of the table.

Sam Panapa, who played for the Eagles in the first season, had been the first Kiwi to join the club. He returned in 1990 for a second season as an established international who had played in all three tests against Great Britain that summer. He scored 14 tries in the campaign before leaving to go to Salford and later Wigan. He is photographed here scoring the first try of a hat-trick in the 62-16 rout of Hull KR after Eagles were already relegated.

Dale Laughton, with Mick Cook in support, is held up by Workington Town defenders. This action comes from a game in the new streamlined Second Division in October 1991. Workington were also challengers for promotion, and the 28-14 Eagles win was one of nine consecutive victories in the Autumn which took them to the top of the table. Dale was the first player in the Eagles first team squad actually from South Yorkshire, having played his early football with Dodworth ARLFC in Barnsley.

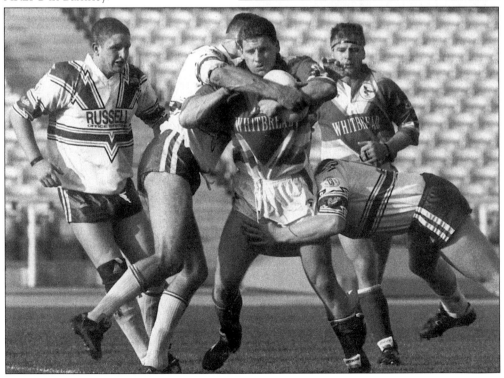

Ruth Beck, the oldest Eagles supporter, celebrates Christmas 1991 with Gary Hetherington at the Don Valley Stadium. This charming lady had first supported Eagles at Owlerton in the late 1980s and went to virtually every home match and most away matches in the next decade. She died just days after the Eagles won the Cup in 1998, at eighty-seven years of age. She'd watched the match on television and had encouraged her team on to the last.

Ian Hughes stops a Scarborough attack in the preliminary round of the Regal Trophy in November 1991. The Pirates only existed for one season, but although defeated 36-8 by the Eagles they by no means disgraced themselves. Ian Hughes, a utility forward with some real pace who joined the club from East Leeds ARLFC, made 107 appearances for the Eagles between 1991 and 1996, scoring 35 tries. He also gained two under-21 Great Britain caps whilst with the club.

Daryll Powell breaks through the French defence in the 1992 international match. Although he was playing in the Second Division, Powell was selected for Great Britain and became a regular member of the GB squad for the rest of the nineties. Altogether he gained 28 Great Britain and 3 England caps whilst with the Eagles before moving on to Keighley in 1995. He subsequently joined Leeds Rhinos and re-joined the Great Britain squad for the 1998 New Zealand tour of Britain. He gained a Cup Winners medal when Leeds won the 1999 Rugby League Challenge Cup at Wembley.

Iva Ropati walks away from scoring despite having had his shorts ripped from him. The crowd were amazed to see the Kiwi centre canter in for his try against Workington wearing only turquoise swimming trunks. Eagles won 48-8 and Ropati, soon to become a New Zealand international, scored 30 tries in the season, which is still a club record. Iva didn't complete the season as he left to go to Oldham in April. He was swapped for fellow Kiwi and ex-All Black Charlie McAllister, who scored 10 tries in the six remaining games.

Aston and Broadbent hoist the Second Division Bowl after beating Ryedale-York 42-7 at the Don Valley on 19 April 1992. Between them is Daryl Powell (in the tracksuit top), who had led the side throughout the season but was serving a rare suspension at the time. Richard Price is on the left of the photograph. Six years later at Wembley in 1998 Broadbent and Aston would be together again in a famous photograph holding an altogether more important trophy.

Eagles players celebrate winning the Second Division Championship with a playing record of played 28, won 21, lost 6 and drawn 1, gaining 43 points. Celebrating the success, from left to right, back row: Young, McAllister, Farrell, Broadbent, Hughes, Plange, Laughton, Mumby, Waddell, Cook, Powell, Robertson. Front row: Shelford, Mycoe, Picksley, Aston, Gamson, Price.

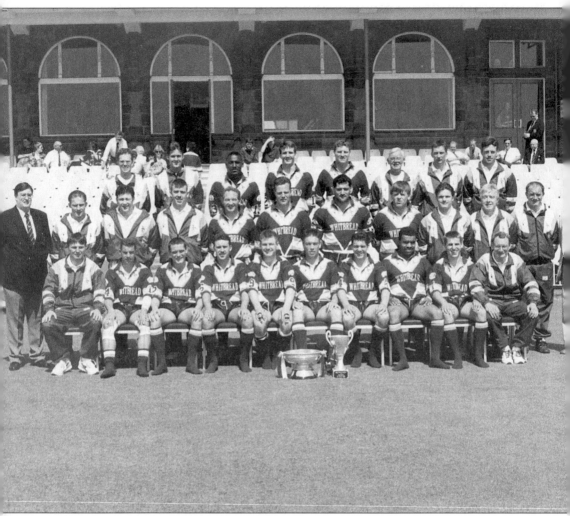

The team was photographed in front of the Old Trafford cricket pavilion where they had been preparing before the Premiership final. Perhaps their boots had not yet arrived? Tim Lumb, who scored a crucial try when the scores were level at 20-20 and turned the game around for Eagles, is seated next to Gary Hetherington on the left of the front row. Only Tim, Mick Cook and Daryl Powell had not played against Ryedale-York when they won the other trophy, the Second Division Championship Bowl, which stands in front of the team in this photograph.

Eagles completed the season by winning the Premiership play-off at Old Trafford in May against Oldham. Here, the three key men, Daryl Powell, Gary Hetherington and Mark Aston, parade the trophy having seen off Oldham by 34-20. Powell got a hat-trick (as he had done in the 1989 final against Swinton at the same ground) and won the Man of the Match Trophy.

Tony Tuimavave joined Eagles from the Northcote club in New Zealand in October 1992 and went straight into his first game against Rochdale when Eagles won 35-14. A hard running, hard tackling forward he played 21 games, scoring 13 tries, that season. Paul Carr, who was to become an Eagles legend, replaced him the following year. Tony went on to star for Auckland Warriors in the Australian Rugby League Competition.

The Lord Mayor, Councillor Bill Jordan, put on a civic reception at the Town Hall to celebrate the Championship and the Premiership win and mark Eagles' return to the First Division. From left to right: Keith Mumby, Hugh Waddell, Anderson 'AJ' Okiwe, Craig Robertson, Paul Broadbent, The Lord Mayor, Mark Aston, David Plange, Richard Picksley, Gary Hetherington.

Four
Up Where We Belong
1992-95

Eagles played Australia in a fixture arranged as part of the Kangeroos' pre-1992 World Cup preparations. For a club that was only eight years old and had just been promoted, to play the World's premier team was an unbelievable dream. Eagles had just reached the Yorkshire Cup final after a good start to their 1992/93 season and saw this game as a great honour, as well as an opportunity to market the club and Rugby League in South Yorkshire. Australia won 52-22 on the night of course, but not before Eagles had scored four tries against them – very few teams would do that against Australia in the 1990s!

Mark Aston models the new yellow Eagles kit. One of the key players in Eagles' history he joined the club from Selby in 1986 although he was born and bred in Castleford, like so many of the top Eagles players during the club's first decade. By the end of the 1999 Super League IV season he had scored 2,103 points from 51 tries, 928 goals and 43 drop goals. He already had one Great Britain appearance against France and earlier in the summer of 1992 he had joined the Great Britain touring party in Australia and New Zealand.

Mark in action against St Helens at the Don Valley Stadium in September 1992. Eagles lost a hard fought game 18-10, with David Plange scoring two tries.

Garry Jack side-stepping the Australian No. 9 Kerrod Walters in the October game at the Don Valley (Australia wore a white strip for their preparatory games). Arguably the most famous player ever to have played for Eagles, Garry was a legend in the game when he came to the UK for one season after his eleven year career ended at Balmain. Garry, who had won all the honours in the game at full-back for Australia, NSW and Balmain, was persuaded to join Eagles by Kath Hetherington over in Australia on a hunt for player-talent. He continued his fine form for Eagles, receiving the 'Full-back of the Year' award in England as well as Australia. He scored 8 tries in his 33 games for Eagles before moving on to Salford in 1993 as player-coach.

David Plange joined Eagles in 1991 from Castleford. He had already made one international appearance when he scored a try against France at Headingley in 1988, not to mention playing for Great Britain against the Rest of the World in 1988 as part of the celebration for the opening of the new Rugby League Hall of Fame. He was an important signing for the Eagles with 98 tries for Castleford already under his belt when he arrived at the Don Valley (after being swapped for Dave Nelson). In his three seasons with the Eagles he would add 84 tries and kick one goal. A very popular player, his hard-running, hard-tackling wing play won him many fans. In the 1992/93 season he topped the try-scoring list (with 18) before his season was cut short by injury.

Hugh Waddell attempts to burst through the Wigan defence whilst being held by Dennis Betts and Mick Cassidy. Ian Hughes and Mark Gamson are the players looking on. Gary Hetherington asked the Rugby League for a home game against Wigan as the first match of the new return season. Most clubs tried to avoid Wigan but Hetherington saw it as a great marketing opportunity. The good news was that 6,000 supporters turned up, but the bad news was that they saw Eagles heavily defeated 46-6.

The Eagles team in the 1992/93 season. From left to right, back row: McGuire, Carr, Hughes, Reilly, Broadbent, Laughton, Farrell, Cook, Jack. Front row: Sheridan, Price, Powell, Aston, Gamson, Stott, A.N. Other (mascot of the day).

Paul Broadbent looking for the off-load in Eagles' home game against Castleford in October 1992. Eagles won 20-16 in a match considered by Eagles as a 'derby' fixture. This was because a considerable number of Sheffield players, like Broadbent himself, came from the Castleford area. For much of the early nineties almost all the coaching staff came from this West Yorkshire mining town as well.

Eagles had opened a club shop in the centre of Sheffield to market the game to a seemingly reluctant Sheffield public. Here, five girls, who were all members of the successful Junior Eagles girls' team, model the 1992 shirt and one from past seasons.

Eagles' saddest day in the 1992/93 season was their defeat in the 'last' Yorkshire Cup final at Elland Road. Here, Kath Hetherington leads out the Eagles – another first for women in Rugby League – followed by husband Gary. Sir Rodney Walker, the chairman of Trinity and later chairman of the Rugby Football League and the Sports Council, leads out the Wakefield side. Eagles were for once the favourites to take the handsome trophy. However, they fell foul of a splendid display by young Nigel Wright and flopped to a disappointing 29-16 defeat. If Eagles had won they would have kept the trophy permanently, but they had played Australia four days before and that game as well as a crowded fixture list had taken their toll on the players.

Mick Cook evading two Wakefield tacklers during the game. Mick Cook was 'Mr Reliable' for Eagles. He demonstrated a tremendous commitment to the club for a decade after joining from Queens ARLFC in Leeds in 1987. He was voted the Players' Player of the Year for four consecutive seasons. A prodigious tackler, he made 259 appearances for the club, scoring 22 tries. For a brief period in 1997 he was Eagles' assistant coach before he left to become part of the coaching staff at Bramley.

Garry Jack (standing in the foreground), Farrell, Carr, Price and Laughton sum up the Eagles players' feelings as Wakefield go up for the cup.

Paul Carr in action against Wakefield in a league match in March 1993, when Eagles gained revenge for their earlier Yorkshire Cup defeat by beating Trinity 26-19. Paul had come to England from South Sydney the year before and had a dramatic season with Hunslet. He scored 26 tries for the Parksiders before being snapped up by the Eagles as they returned to the First Division. Paul was one of the best signings the club ever made and the longest serving and most effective Australian to have turned out in Sheffield's colours.

Ian Hughes and Andy Young 'keep in touch' in one of the late season games. Eagles finished the 1992/93 season with their best First Division performance yet. Their record was P26 W10 D1 L15, with a final position of tenth.

Sheffield did get to Wembley in 1993, but it was the Sheffield Schools under-11s that graced the Twin Towers in the pre-Cup Final schools game. The team was coached by Ian Anniss (pictured in the centre of the rear rank) and played Rochdale in the Wembley game. They lost narrowly, but demonstrated that Rugby League was establishing itself in the 'Steel City' and that a solid foundation for the game was being laid in the schools and amateur junior ranks. Wigan, of course, won the grown-up final.

Daryl Powell models Eagles ground-breaking new 1993/94 shirt. No hoops or big chevrons now, but a screaming Eagle swooping across the front of the shirt. Perhaps the Eagle was having its parts refreshed as the club struck a new deal with sponsors Whitbread to market the Heineken lager brand.

There was a new coach for the season: Eagles succumbed to ACS (Australian Coach Syndrome) and appointed Bill Gardner of the Brisbane Broncos to take over from Gary Hetherington and Steve Ferres. Gary stayed on as manager, chairman and everything else, but Gardner took over the team. Many players benefited from his Australian coaching style and rated him as a coach. 'Bronco Bill', as he was nicknamed, saw that his first task was to build up the squad and develop its skills over two or three years. A run of defeats before Christmas however (including a Regal Trophy 8-6 defeat at Batley), caused the directors to re-think the coaching situation. They re-installed Gary Hetherington and Bill Gardner spent that Christmas in Australia. Hetherington's first match back in charge saw a 28-22 win over Salford on 22 December and the season picked up from there on.

If there was no 'V' on the shirt then the players could form one for this pre-season team photograph taken in August 1993. From left to right: James, Farrell, Grimoldby, Broadbent,

Stott, Sheridan, Price, Cook, Gamson, Powell, Lumb, Picksley, Aston, Mycoe, McGuire, Carr, Plange, Hughes, Fraisse. Once again, the boots do not seem to have arrived yet.

Eagles made a major signing one month into the new season. Lee Jackson, already a top class international hooker, came to Sheffield for £83,000 from Hull FC, his home-town club. Hetherington helped to pay for his new star by undertaking a sponsored run to St Helens (although not in one day) in time for an Eagles away match. Lee Jackson soon showed his class and was re-selected for Great Britain in the test series against New Zealand and France. Here, he is pictured with his family just after signing for the club.

A section of Eagles' faithful away supporters. Many of the most familiar of Eagles fans are in this picture taken on the Oldham terraces. In the centre Kath Owen is leading the cheering with her drum (it got bigger in subsequent seasons), with a young Lucy Hetherington on the bodhran.

Paul Carr breaks into open play in Eagles 11-20 home defeat against Castleford. Giving chase is Tawera Nikau, who played ten games for Eagles in 1990 after touring with the Kiwis. Although unknown in England, he made a big impression with Eagles fans and scored 5 tries in his brief stay. He was made a big offer to go to York in the close season of 1990 and later played for Castleford before returning down under to international honours and a career with several ARL clubs.

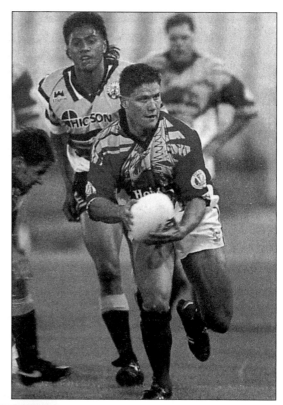

Eagles had an indifferent period in the run up to Christmas 1993. So, when a group of players visited Santa in his grotto he presented them with 'A WIN', the gift they needed the most. Santa's magic worked because Eagles beat Salford three days before Christmas. Receiving this 'priceless' present (from left to right) at the rear are David Fraisse and Paul Carr, with Mark Aston and Lynton Stott thanking the bearded one. Dale Laughton may have had some Christmas spirit already because he has slumped to the floor, whilst Santa himself looks decidedly bibulous.

Bruce McGuire storms through the Leigh defence in the fourth round of the 1994 Rugby League Challenge Cup. Bruce was one of Eagles' most successful Australian signings and he was enjoying his second spell with the club, having played in the 1989/90 season and returning when he finished his Balmain career in 1992. He was capped twice for Australia, both times against New Zealand, and played 78 games for Eagles, scoring 9 tries, before going on to Warrington in 1994.

Finally, on 17 March 1994, Eagles beat Wigan, the club of the decade. Although it was a close match, Eagles were consistently the better side and won 10-5. The club felt it had come of age as Mark Aston got the Eagles' points with a try and three goals. The picture shows Mark seconds after he has grounded the ball for his second-half try that won the game. In Eagles' three previous games with Wigan they had conceded 130 points. It was the best win in Eagles' history since the 1989 victory over World Cup champions, Widnes, at Bramall Lane.

A bad hair day for Bruce McGuire as he combines with Ian Hughes to snuff out another Wigan attack and keep Eagles on the winning track.

Richard Picksley almost scored a second try for Eagles' but was cut down inches from the line by a magnificent tackle from Gary Connolly, the Wigan international centre. Eagles had been playing so well that the win was not entirely unexpected. Four years later they would achieve a more incredible result when they beat Wigan 17-8 in the 1998 Rugby League Challenge Cup final at Wembley.

Eagles players and officials celebrate the end of their most successful league season yet after their 21-6 home defeat of Widnes. They finished sixth in the table with 16 wins and 2 draws from 30 games. This got them into the play-offs for the first time.

David Fraisse, Eagles' first-ever French signing, is welcomed by Mark Aston and Daryl Powell as he joins the club for the beginning of the 1993/94 season. David was introduced to the Eagles by Glenn Knight, the assistant coach, who had coached in France. He was already an established French international, having scored in France's unexpected test victory at Headingley in 1990. He would play four more times for France as an Eagles player and be followed to the club by Freddy Banquet, Laurent Lucchese and Jean-Marc Garcia.

David Fraisse heads for the try-line in the semi-finals of the 1994 Premiership pursued by Wigan's Simon Haughton. Although Eagles got three tries in their 52-18 defeat, Wigan completely dominated the middle period of the game and finished Eagles' hopes of a return to an Old Trafford Premiership final.

The Featherstone Rovers programme for their home match with Eagles shows Mark Aston in the Rovers colours. Unhappy with the contract offered to him, Mark had been transferred at the end of the 1993/94 season. He spent an unsuccessful season at Featherstone and was soon back at Sheffield for the Centenary season. There, his career took off again, culminating in winning the Lance Todd Trophy at Wembley in May 1998.

Daryl Powell (on the left in the tracksuit) with some of the Eagles team who played in his testimonial match against Castleford in August 1994. Eagles sported their new green strip with a black Eagle, the sixth colour in which they had played. From left to right, back row: Hutchinson, Hughes, Thompson, Laughton, Hayes. Front row: Gamson, Carr, Price, Farrell, Briggs, Picksley.

'I'm right behind you mate.' Paul Broadbent backs up Lee Jackson at a play-the-ball against Hull in October 1994. Eagles won 38-14 and Broadbent got one of the tries.

Anthony Farrell crashes through the Warrington defence to score, despite the attentions of Jonathan Davies and Greg Mackey, in September 1994. Eagles won this game at the Don Valley 29-8.

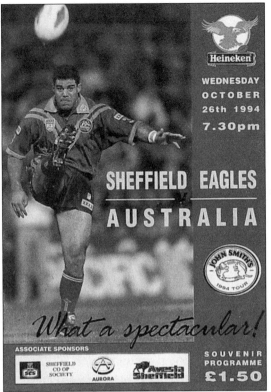

Mal Meninga featured on the front of the programme for the club's second encounter with Australia. The opportunity to play the Kangaroos was won on merit this time, as Eagles had finished sixth in the league the season before. Heavily promoted, Eagles looked forward to a spectacular evening. They got one – but not as planned! Australia had lost the First Test to Great Britain at Wembley the Saturday before and turned out an almost full strength side who demolished Eagles 80-2.

Paul Carr tackles fellow Australian Terry Hill of Canterbury aided by David Mycoe. The Eagles players took such a battering that their changing room resembled a casualty clearing station as the Aussies recorded their biggest win in England since the 1920s.

Darrell Trindall arrived from South Sydney and appeared to have become acclimatised to our weather. He played one game against Workington in early September, where he played well and kicked three goals. However, he was next heard of aboard a Qantas plane heading down under and never appeared for Eagles again. He subsequently played top grade Rugby League for South Sydney but he remained Eagles briefest ever overseas signing.

Bright Sodje joined the club from Hull KR, where he was a prolific try-scorer. British-born of Nigerian parents, he was swapped for David Plange in the 1994 close season. He had played Rugby Union with Blackheath before changing codes and ended the 1994/95 season with 10 tries. He scored another 10 in the short Centenary season in 1995/96. Like Plange, he was to become a popular player with the Eagles supporters.

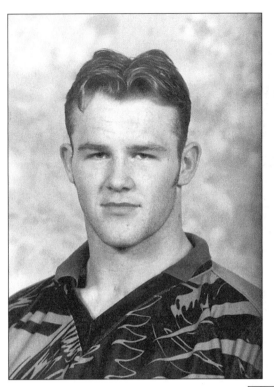

Keith Senior signed for the Eagles in 1994 after playing with their academy side. Huddersfield-born, he took a while to settle into the squad but his career took off in the 1996 Super League season when he scored 17 tries. This gained him selection for the 1996 Oceania Tour with the Great Britain squad where he gained two caps against Fiji and New Zealand. One of the most exciting centres in the modern game, he played in all three tests against New Zealand in 1998. Near to the end of the 1999 season, he was transferred to Leeds Rhinos, whose squad has a sizeable ex-Eagles contingent.

Laurent Lucchese joined Eagles just before Christmas 1994. A very classy full-back, he added composure in defence and an attacking flair that strengthened the team. A serious injury at the end of the season cut short his Eagles career, although he did gain two French international caps whilst with the club. His next encounter with the Sheffield Eagles was on the opening night of the Super League on 29 March 1996 in the Charlety Stadium, when he represented the new Paris St Germain team as they edged Eagles 30-24.

Eagles have been well served by volunteers over the years. Rather than have a traditional supporters club, who often can do everything but help, Hetherington set up a group of supporters who carried out vital matchday tasks. Pictured above are key helpers known to all Eagles. Fans, from left to right: Don Powell, Lynda Wood, Tony Roberts, Joan Roberts, Barry Minshell, Julie Bush (club secretary), Kevin O'Kane, Brian Appleton.

Ryan Sheridan makes a characteristic break for the try-line. Now Aston had left to play for Featherstone, Ryan got his chance in the first team and made a sensational impact. He already had 4 Great Britain Academy Caps and in 1994 represented the GB under-21s against Australia. He was a product of the Eagles' scouting and academy system, having signed in 1991 from Dewsbury Moor ARLFC. He left in 1997 to follow Gary Hetherington to Leeds and was a contender for the Lance Todd Trophy in the 1999 Rugby League Cup final – the last ever held at the old Wembley Stadium.

Paul Carr slams home for a typical try. From ten yards out Paul's determination was phenomenal. This score was against Leigh in December 1994 in the Regal Trophy, which Eagles won 46-10. They were to meet Leigh regularly in cup competitions in the 1990s.

Kath Hetherington became the first woman to become the president of the Rugby Football League. She is shown here wearing the famous chain of office shortly after taking the position for the Centenary year. No one now doubted Kath's credentials to hold the post, as she was clearly recognised as one of the most knowledgeable people in the professional game. She held the presidency for two seasons (in 1995 and 1996) at a time of great celebration and tremendous change for the game.

With the advent of Super League the Rugby Football League attempted to encourage neighbouring clubs to merge. This policy was resisted in all areas but Gary Hetherington was seriously prepared to consider a merger with Doncaster. They had finally made the top division in 1994 and had virtually bankrupted themselves trying to match the higher playing standard. Their board was receptive to the idea of a merger, but their fans were not. This photograph from March 1995 shows the Dons' director John Sheridan and captain Dave Evans with Hetherington and Powell at a time when a merger looked likely. Subsequently, the teams went their own separate ways and the Dons became the Dragons and moved out of Tattersfield forever.

Sonny Whakarau (left) was one Doncaster player who moved over to the Eagles as the teams moved into the Centenary season. A Kiwi prop with a considerable reputation, he only played 8 games for the Eagles before moving on. Here, he is photographed with Andy Hay, recently signed from Castleford for £70,000. Andy had gained a Great Britain under-21 cap before coming to Eagles and was regarded as a player of great potential. In his three years with Eagles he never quite reached that promise, but since he followed Gary Hetherington to Leeds in 1997 he has blossomed as a second row forward of international standard.

71

Brian Aston, Eagles' commercial manager for most of the 1990s, launched a new lottery scheme called Super Loot. He is shown here signing up Paul Broadbent to the venture. Brian is the father of Mark Aston and had been a formative influence in young Mark's junior playing career before joining Eagles. Paul became the new captain of Eagles after Daryl Powell had left to join Keighley Cougars. Daryl had been captain since 1986 and had appeared to be a permanent fixture at the club. Paul would be an effective captain for the next four seasons and he also gained international honours with 8 Great Britain and 5 England Caps to his credit.

Darren Turner, 'Rocky' to all his friends and a few of his enemies as well, joined the Eagles Academy from the Huddersfield amateur club Paddock ARLFC. A fearsome forward, he gained selection to the 1999 England squad. Probably his biggest moment in Rugby League was scoring the decisive third try at Wembley in the 1998 Rugby League Challenge Cup final.

The Eagles team for the 1995/96 Centenary season at their pre-season photo-call. From left to right, back row: Peter Regan (assistant coach), Farrell, Gamson, Lawford, Lawless, Senior, Sodje. Middle row: Young, Hay, Hughes, Whakarau, Carr, Picksley, Turner. Front row: Alan Tomlinson (physiotherapist), Sheridan, Price, Hetherington, Broadbent, Ted Dowde (team manager), Mycoe, Stott, Peter Tate (team assistant).

Gary Hetherington with his assistant coach Peter Regan. Australian-born Regan had joined Eagles from Rochdale Hornets and at the end of the Centenary season he would move on to coach Batley.

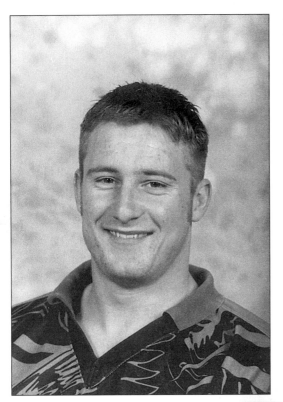

Lynton Stott was the first ever Lancastrian signed by Eagles when he joined the club in 1992 from Woolston Rovers ARLFC in Warrington. A gutsy winger or full-back he never gave less than 100% effort and in an Eagles career that lasted 130 matches he scored 56 tries and kicked 12 goals. In 1999 he moved on to Super League new boys Wakefield Trinity, where he continues to notch up the tries for the Wildcats.

Mark Aston concentrates on an 'up and under' as Kevin Langer of the newly restyled London Broncos approaches for the tackle in a game at the Don Valley that ended in a 42-10 victory for the Londoners. Bought out by the fabulously successful Brisbane Broncos, the team wore the Queensland club's strip for their first season before they were fast-tracked into Super League I. Aussie influences on the game were beginning to re-name the high attacking kick as a 'bomb' – Eddie 'Up and Under' Waring would no doubt be turning in his grave.

Danny McAllister looks wistfully up at the Don Valley Stadium after joining Eagles in October 1995. He was then twenty-one and had played with the South Queensland Crushers in the 1995 Winfield Cup competition. He played for two and a half seasons before returning to Australia and joining the Gold Coast Chargers. In 1999 he returned to Britain to play first with Bramley and then with the new Super League franchise, the Gateshead Thunder.

Mick Cook powers through a tackle in the game against Halifax in February 1996. Mick had rediscovered a role for himself as a hard-tackling prop forward and his commitment was as great as ever. In the summer of 1995 he had played for Wagga Wagga in the NSW Country League and on his return became an assistant coach with the Eagles.

After the Centenary World Cup held in October 1995, Eagles signed three members of the Fijian squad. Joe Dakuitoga (a winger who had played for Penrith Panthers in the ARL), Mala Yasa (a former Fijian Rugby Union international) and Waisale Sovatabua. Only Waisale stayed the course and played as a powerful running full-back or winger in all four Super League seasons. Here he is pictured in Fiji's colours in their match against Australia, a game in which he made a big impression on many British Rugby League fans and coaches.

Five

Super League
1996-1999

Rugby League's ambitious re-invention of itself as a high profile, summer sport, backed by Rupert Murdoch's Sky TV, got off to a spectacular start at the Charlety Stadium in Paris on 29 March 1996. Paris St Germain, the newly created French team full of French internationals, played the Eagles in the opening fixture of Super League. As the teams entered the stadium, fireworks erupted from all sides, welcoming the crowds and French and British TV viewers to the new dawn of full-time professional Rugby League.

Eagles had made an important signing in French international three-quarter Jean-Marc Garcia and one of his first duties, along with his wife Catherine, was to translate the Eagles' press releases and send them off to the French press. They are pictured at the fax machine letting all of France know that 'Les Aigles' were coming. The champagne bottle behind adds a topical touch to the photograph, although Stones are not one of the better-known champagne houses!

Playing in Paris in the first ever Super League game was a dream start for Eagles' marketing department. Here, Jean-Marc holds-up the souvenir scarf that many of the Eagles fans took with them for the Paris weekend.

Joe Dakuitoga, the Eagles' Fijian winger, runs onto the pitch alongside his Paris opposite number. Two by two the players entered the stadium flanked by parallel rows of spurting roman candles.

Eagles players make their final preparations before the start of the game. In front are McAllister, Hay, Lawford, Carr and Garcia, whilst Mick Cook at the rear gives some last minute advice.

The two captains shake hands after the game. Patrick Entat, probably the best-known French international player in the UK, had had a successful spell with Hull FC and he led his team with determination. Paul Broadbent looks less excited by the outcome of the match. However, everyone else in the world of Super League was overjoyed. The new Paris St Germain team had proved it could compete with British clubs and they had 18,000 spectators in the stadium watching a game whose heartland was in the south west of the country. Super League officials felt confident that the whole occasion vindicated their vision of Rugby League's future.

Danny McAllister, Jean-Marc Garcia, David Mycoe and Paul Broadbent read through the special Eagles Super League supplement produced by the *Sheffield Star*.

Mick Cook, in a typically determined mood, takes a break from a game. He is wearing the new 1996 away kit that gained wider fame when one of the actors in the very successful film *The Full Monty* wore it in a number of scenes in the movie. Although the shirt was considered very attractive by the fans, it was ditched by the team because they failed to win whilst wearing it.

Anthony Farrell and Lynton Stott keep a sharp eye on London Broncos players as they prepare to play the ball in a match that Eagles won 34-18 at the Don Valley Stadium in April 1996. Eagles were virtually unbeatable in Sheffield in the 1996 season, winning 9 out of 10 games played in the city.

Five Eagles players celebrate Paul Carr's birthday. From left to right: Mick Cook, Dale Laughton, Paul himself, Danny McAllister and Jean-Marc Garcia. Paul only played 12 games in the 1996 season because of a fractured cheekbone. The 1995 reduced Centenary season had been a vintage one for Paul, who had chalked up 10 tries, many of them scored by sheer strength and determination.

Johnny Lawless is stopped after a characteristic scoot from the acting half-back position. This game against St Helens was played at Cardiff Arms Park. It was an Eagles 'home' game but transferred to South Wales to encourage the development of Rugby League in the principality.

Paul Carr and Mark Aston play their part in preparing a superb French dish supervised by master chef Alain Carvo. Despite the player's totally 'authentic' appearance, the berets were army surplus and the onions came from the props department of the Crucible Theatre.

Jean-Marc Garcia, who was a highly qualified chef, shows how it should be done, as he produces an omelette for two Eagles supporters. Keith Senior is also awaiting his turn for a taste.

Angela and Chris Fowler were married on 15 June 1996 – a day that clashed with the return game at the Don Valley against Paris St Germain. No worries! After the service, the newly married couple arrived at the ground at half-time and were ferried to their places on a special wedding mobile complete with balloons, to a tremendous welcome from the fans. Eagles supplied the 'wedding banquet' by trouncing Paris 52-18.

Darren Turner and Lynton Stott combine to end Gary Connolly's attack in Eagles' single defeat in Sheffield in 1996. The tackle looks barely legal but Connolly survived it as Wigan strode home 54-12 in a game played at Bramall Lane.

Richard Chapman receives the Man of the Match award from Clive Betts, then leader of the City Council, later MP for Attercliffe. Peter Sephton, a director of the club and chairman of Mainline Buses, a long time sponsor of the Eagles, looks on. The young scrum half only played one game in 1996 but he scored two tries as Workington were defeated 32-16. In 1998 he would be a key player in Featherstone Rovers team in the FASDA play-off final at the McAlpine Stadium.

Darren Turner heads for the Warrington line leaving Jon Roper standing as Eagles scrape home 28-22 at Bramall Lane. Gary Hetherington wanted the three big games of the season – Leeds, Wigan and Warrington – to be played at Bramall Lane to test whether crowd support would be improved. Once again Eagles were considering a move to one of the big soccer stadiums in the city, where the crowd was closer to the pitch than in the essentially athletics stadium of Don Valley.

The track at Don Valley, however, had other uses. Garcia, Mycoe, Senior and Mala Yasa, the Fijian, are pictured trying out new bikes provided by a new sponsor.

Halifax's Perrett is well tackled by Cook, Farrell and Senior in the last home game of the season. Eagles won 42-28 but lost their two remaining away games. Of the eleven away games in Super League, only the game at Workington in April had a successful outcome: although they heavily defeated the Cumbrians 54-22, they did not manage to win another away game all season.

The crimson flows from Paul Carr's head as the magic fluid is applied to revive him. Although he was the toughest of competitors, this time he had to retire from the Castleford game in May 1996.

Joe Dakuitoga, one of the three Fijians signed by Gary Hetherington after the 1995 World Cup. Joe was the most experienced of the trio, with 3 Rugby League international caps as well as 3 Rugby Union ones. He had played for Penrith Panthers in the Winfield Cup in the 1994 and 1995 seasons and had scored 37 tries in top class rugby before he signed for the Eagles. He played 19 games in two seasons for the Eagles and scored 2 more tries before returning to the Pacific.

Johnny Lawless off-loads as Eagles attack. Johnny came to Eagles from his home-town club Halifax in the summer of 1995. He'd played for their academy team before moving on to their first team and winning 3 Great Britain Academy caps. A robust and hard tackling hooker, he always gave 100% effort for the Eagles and his skills brought him selection for the England sides that played France and Wales in 1996. In his first season with the club (1995/96) he scored 10 tries, making him the joint top scorer with Paul Carr. In 1998 he swapped international jerseys and turned out for Ireland in their games against France and Scotland.

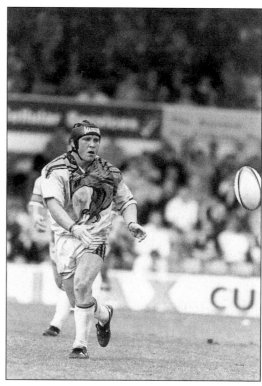

Mark Aston, Lynton Stott and Keith Senior sign autographs after the match. Eagles have always made a special effort to give young supporters access to players. Many have gone on to try Rugby League in their schools or local clubs.

Gary Hetherington welcomes Lawrence Taylor and Curtis Thomas, who signed for Eagles in April 1996 from the fledgling Rugby League club in Leicester. They were key members of the Alliance side for the next two seasons and represented the interest that the Midlands and the South were taking in Rugby League Football.

Paul Daley, Eagles' academy coach, with some of his new academy players in March 1996. From left to right: Dale Cardoza, James Brown, Damien Dean, Ben Cooper and Chris Molyneux. By 1999 Cardoza and Molyneux had both played in the first team whilst Molyneux had gained four Young Lions caps against France.

For several seasons the E-girls were an important part of Eagles pre-match entertainment. Highly skilled dancers, they brought far more panache to the occasion than most teams' cheerleaders. They were led by the Baddon sisters, Nikki and Louise, who are in the middle of the back row.

At the end of the season Freddy the Eagle was unmasked. It was John Smith, sometime chairman of the Eagles Supporters Club. He is pictured here trying to comfort shocked and disappointed fans who thought the birdman was real.

Eagles' final match of the season ended in another disappointing away defeat. They lost 34-25 to Oldham in their last ever visit to the Watersheddings, Oldham's old, famous and very bleak ground. From left to right, back row: Glenn Knight (assistant coach), Maggie Kennett (masseuse), Simon Worsnop (conditioner), Hughes, Taylor, McAllister, Carr, Laughton, Senior, Dixon, Turner, Gary Grienke (assistant coach), Nigel Kent (physiotherapist), Gary Hetherington (coach). Front row: Alan Tomlinson (physiotherapist), Stott, Garcia, Sheridan, Cook, Broadbent (captain), Lawless, Mycoe, Lawford, Aston and Janet Hornbuckle (club doctor). The season had ended with 10 wins out of 22 games and Eagles had attained seventh place. Although no-one else knew it at the time, this August 1996 match was to be Gary Hetherington's last as coach and chairman of the club.

In November 1996 a bombshell hit the Eagles when Gary Hetherington announced he had accepted the post of Chief Executive with Leeds RLFC and was leaving the club he had founded and sustained since 1984. Terry Sharman, seen here with his wife Kathie, took secondment from his own job to cover as temporary chairman and chief executive until the club could fully regain its feet. He had been a director of the Eagles from the very start in 1984 and was currently president of the club. Kathie also had a long close association with the club and she moved up to become the full-time financial director.

At the same time as Hetherington's departure, Phil Larder became the club coach. Larder, who was the current Great Britain coach, was still touring in New Zealand with the Great Britain tour party when the news broke. His appointment was regarded as a coup for the Eagles, especially as he was joined by John Kear as his assistant. Many supporters felt that Gary Hetherington had gone as far as he could as coach and his conflicting roles within the club were effecting his efficiency. Larder's reign, however, was to be short-lived and somewhat unexpectedly he ended the year as part of the coaching team of the England Rugby Union squad.

The new face of Eagles for the 1997 Super League II season. From left to right, back row: Sodje, Pinkney, Flynn, Garcia, Crowther, Doyle, Taewa, Morganson, Sovatabua. Middle row: John Kear (assistant coach), Turner, Dixon, Laughton, Edmed, Thompson, McAllister, Hay, Wood, Mycoe, Maggie Kennet (conditioner). Front row: Stott, Carr, Aston, Phil Larder (coach), Broadbent (captain), Terry Sharman (chairman), Cook, Senior, Lawless.

Four new players who joined in 1997 salute the crowd. They are, from left to right: Whetu Taewa (the Kiwi international who joined from North Queensland Cowboys), Martin Wood and Nick Pinkney (who had been Larder's stars at Keighley Cougars) and Marcus Vassilakopoulos (who, despite having the longest name in Rugby League, was a Hull lad and joined the club from Leeds). Marcus was the youngest forward to play at Wembley when he turned out for Leeds *v.* Wigan in the 1994 Cup Final.

Steve Edmed had played nine years for Balmain Tigers before moving to North Queensland in 1996. A prop with a big reputation down under, he played 20 games for Eagles before sustaining a serious neck injury which put him out of action for the last third of the season. He recovered for the 1998 season but in his first game back at Castleford suffered knee ligament damage and his Eagles career sadly came to an end.

Eagles
Plc

(Incorporated and registered in England and Wales under the Companies Act 1985 with Registration No 3350848)

OFFER

of 2,250,000 ordinary shares of 5p each at 40p per share

and Admission to the Alternative Investment Market

Nominated adviser and nominated broker to the Company

PEEL, HUNT & COMPANY LIMITED

SHARE CAPITAL IMMEDIATELY FOLLOWING THE OFFER

Authorised			Issued and fully paid	
Number	*Amount (£)*		*Number*	*Amount (£)*
20,000,000	1,000,000	ordinary shares of 5p each	9,750,000	487,500

The Offer, which is fully underwritten, is conditional, *inter alia*, on Admission taking place on or before 21 May 1997 (or such later date as the Company and Peel Hunt may agree). The Offer Shares will rank in full for all dividends or other distributions hereafter declared, made or paid on the ordinary share capital of the Company and will rank *pari passu* in all other respects with all other Ordinary Shares which will be in issue on Admission.

Peel Hunt has been appointed as nominated adviser and nominated broker to the Company and acts for no one else in relation to the Offer and will not be responsible to any other person for providing the protections afforded to customers of Peel Hunt or for providing advice in relation to the Offer. In accordance with the AIM Rules, Peel Hunt expects to confirm to the London Stock Exchange that it has satisfied itself that the Directors have received advice and guidance as to the nature of their responsibilities and obligations to ensure compliance by the Company with the AIM Rules and that, to the best of its knowledge and belief, all relevant requirements of the AIM Rules have been complied with. Peel Hunt has not made its own enquiries except as to matters which have come to its attention and on which it considered it necessary to satisfy itself. No liability whatsoever is accepted by Peel Hunt for the accuracy of any information or opinions contained in this document or for the omission of any material information, for which the Directors are solely responsible.

The Directors of Eagles plc, whose names appear on page 3 of this document, accept responsibility for the information contained in this document, including individual and collective responsibility for compliance with the AIM Rules. To the best of the knowledge and belief of the Directors (who have taken all reasonable care to ensure that such is the case), the information contained in this document is in accordance with the facts and does not omit anything likely to affect the import of such information. In making a decision whether or not to invest in the Offer, no information or representation should be relied upon in relation to the Offer, the Company or the Ordinary Shares, save as contained in this document. No person has been authorised to give any information or make any representation save as contained in this document and, if given or made, such information or representation must not be relied upon as having been authorised.

Eagles plc became the first Rugby League club to be floated on the Stock Exchange. The new owner, Paul Thompson of Sanderson Electronics, wanted to improve the capitalisation of the club and so this prospectus was launched in April 1997 on the Alternative Investment Market of the London Stock Exchange. A staggering $2\frac{1}{4}$ million shares were on offer to supporters and many took advantage of the opportunity to own part of their club.

After all the hype surrounding the club's new owners, new chief executive and new coaching team, the first Super League game of the season was an anti-climax. Once again it was against Paris St Germain, but this time the game was in Sheffield. Eagles, despite all their new signings – including Steve Edmed (pictured in the front row prior to the scrum going down) – looked rather ordinary and lost 18-4 to the Frenchmen.

Mark Aston and Lynton Stott celebrate – or perhaps drown their sorrows – after a home game early in the season. The new red shirt was not universally popular and was usually referred to as the Arsenal strip. However, if fans wanted to be particularly unkind they called it the Rotherham United shirt. The club also had a new logo featuring a more ferocious looking Eagle on the centre of the top.

Young Eagles fans model nine of the 1997 shirts of the Super League teams. From left to right: Bradford, Salford, Warrington, Wigan, Leeds, Eagles, Halifax, Castleford and St Helens.

Rod Doyle was the fourth Australian signing by Phil Larder for the 1997 season and the only one to continue into the 1999 Super League IV season. Queensland born, he played for St George Dragons and Eastern Suburbs in Sydney in the first half of the 1990s before joining South Queensland Crushers in 1996. In three seasons (1997-1999) he would play 74 games for Eagles, including the Wembley Cup Final, and score 13 tries, usually from the back row.

Rod Doyle scores against Castleford in April 1997 in one of the few wins during Phil Larder's reign as coach. Eagles beat the Tigers 42-20.

Two weeks later Eagles went down to Leeds (now improbably called the Rhinos) 30-18. Here, Matt Crowther is pictured tackling the young Leroy Rivett. Almost two years to the day, Rivett would win the Lance Todd Trophy and create a new Wembley record as he notched four tries in Leeds' 1999 Cup Final win over London Broncos. Rod Doyle looks on as the tackle is completed.

In May, the Eagles directors decided that they needed a new coach and Phil Larder left the club. Like Gardner in 1993, he had not produced a winning team, although some of the defeats – notably against Halifax, Salford and Oldham – had been very close. John Kear now stepped up to take the top job. He was already well qualified with years of coaching experience at Rugby Football League Headquarters, Lions tours to Australia and New Zealand and a spell in 1996 rescuing Paris St Germain. He looks apprehensive at the news of his appointment but appears to be sprouting wings that perhaps account for the next twelve months amazing success for Eagles and himself.

Eagles met Perth Reds in the ambitious Anglo-Australian World Club Cup competition played in the summer of 1997 in Britain and Australia. Paul Broadbent leads his team out flanked by the Cross of St George and the Southern Cross.

Eagles players celebrate on the podium after the match. After some of the massive defeats handed out to top British sides like St Helens and Bradford, Eagles' victory seemed even more remarkable and John Kear's methods and discipline were beginning to bear fruit. The Reds got their revenge in Perth in July when Eagles lost 48-12.

The second time Eagles played in the World Club Cup Competition their opponents were Hunter Mariners, who eventually reached the final. A new Super League Club in Newcastle NSW, they only lasted one year but, under coach Graham Murray, they were a formidable team. In this action shot Eagles and Mariners stretch for a high 'bomb'. The Australians were much too good for the Sheffielders and won comfortably 40-4.

Where did that one go? Kevin Iro, the much travelled New Zealand and Cook Island international, slings out a pass that has the Eagles' sliding defence scrambling to cover. From left to right: Pinkney, Taewa, Senior, Carr and Aston are looking concerned.

Martin Wood and Steve Edmed halt a Saints attack as Chris Joynt offers gentle support. Eagles usually did well against St Helens in Sheffield and this game was no exception as they won a close match 14-12.

Following the win against the Saints, Was Sovatabua leads the community signing as his sceptical colleagues look on.

Freddie the Eagle now had a son, Kid-E. Together they brought free milk from Super League to the fans whilst 'Big Kev' in the background keeps an eye on the players' entrance.

Dave Watson, the much-travelled Kiwi international, returned to Britain in the spring of 1998 and joined Eagles. His never-say-die approach to attack and defence endeared him to the Sheffield fans and his performance in the Wembley final almost won him the Lance Todd Trophy. He first came to the UK in 1987 and gained 15 New Zealand caps against all the International Board members.

The coaching triumvirate of Steve Deakin, John Kear and conditioner Simon Worsnop, pictured here before the 1998 season. They were soon to gain national fame as the coaching staff who planned the defeat of Wigan in the 1998 Rugby League Challenge Cup final. John Kear himself had already been appointed the French national coach in September 1997 and by the end of 1998 season he would be made the assistant coach to the Great Britain team for the three tests against New Zealand. Subsequently, in the spring of 1999, he would be chosen as the England coach for the two 1999 games against France.

There were changes in the Eagles boardroom and senior management as Tim Adams replaced Terry Sharman as chairman. Adams had been on the Eagles board during 1997 and in November was asked by Paul Thompson to take the chair and bring new direction to the club's strategies, both on and off the field. Leeds born, he had been a Rugby League fan from his earliest days and his career with Lonrho in Africa and the UK brought major league business experience to the Eagles. In May 1999 this expertise was further recognised when his colleagues at Super League Europe brought him onto their board of directors. At the end of the season he led the club into a controversial merger with Huddersfield Giants.

Ralph Rimmer, a former Great Britain Students international forward, had been Sheffield's development officer since 1994. It was Terry Sharman who realised the potential of this Liverpool University graduate and promoted him as general manager in 1997. His ability to appreciate all aspects of the Rugby League game from juniors, amateurs and Super League brought him an invitation to join the Eagles board as chief executive in July 1998. Belfast born, he was selected in May 1999 as the manager of the Irish national squad for the forthcoming 1999 Home International Championship.

Steve Molloy joined Eagles in February 1998 after a long period of negotiations with Featherstone Rovers. Because of this he was cup-tied and missed the Wembley final. He already had 4 Great Britain caps and 3 for England as a prop forward when he joined Eagles. He was then selected to captain the Emerging England side that gained a 15-14 victory over Wales at Widnes in July 1998. He is seen here before the start of the game with Keith Senior, who also played in the England team that day. Gareth Stephens and Martin Pearson starred for Wales in the same match.

There was a new sponsor for the 1998 season. LG, the Korean electronics giant, agreed to sponsor the club for two years and the players are pictured here sampling their wares. From left to right: Aston, Taewa, Laughton and Broadbent carry off a wide-screen television set.

The 1998 team that made Eagles history poses for the official photograph before the start of the season. From left to right, back row: Caroline Wellington (masseuse), Gareth Stephens, Michael Jackson, Dave Watson, Whetu Taewa, Bright Sodje, Neil Law, Nick Pinkney, Wayne Flynn, Waisale Sovatabua, Lynton Stott, Alan Tomlinson (physiotherapist). Middle row: Janet Hornbuckle (doctor), Steve Deakin (assistant coach), Martin Wood, Steve Molloy, Rod Doyle, Marcus Vassilakopoulos, Darren Shaw, Ricky Wright, Darren Turner, Simon Worsnop (conditioner), Shaun Matthewman (kit manager). Front Row: Matt Crowther, Dale Laughton, Mark Aston, John Kear (coach), Paul Broadbent (captain), Tim Adams (chairman), Paul Carr, Keith Senior, Johnny Lawless. They are wearing the Eagles' new red, white and blue strip that first made its appearance towards the end of the 1997 season. This kit became known universally as the 'Pepsi shirt', because of the similarity to the logo of a well known US soft drinks company.

Another fans' day out as Castleford and Eagles supporters vie for who can look the daftest in an all-male skirt or kilt competition. The significance of the large teapot is now lost in the mists of time.

Keith Senior strides home for a try pursued by two ex-Eagles, Ryan Sheridan and Anthony Farrell, as Eagles lose a close encounter with Leeds 23-24 at the Don Valley in May 1998. It was an Iestyn Harris last minute penalty from inside his own half that robbed Eagles of the lead they had held throughout the game.

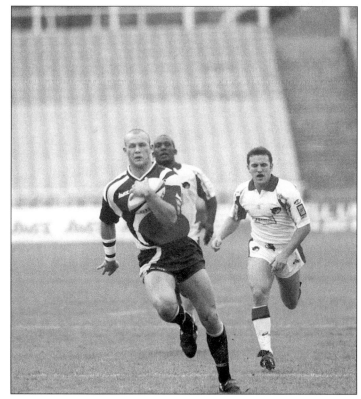

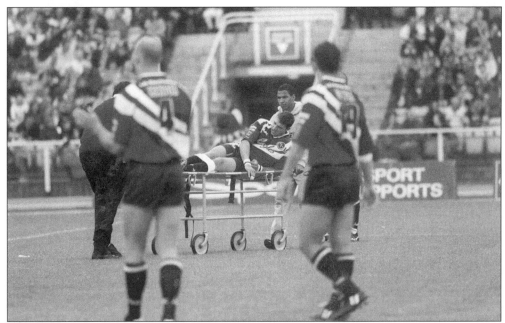

The sad sight of Matt Crowther being carried off from the Leeds game after he had seriously damaged a knee ligament. He had been in tremendous form in 1998 and at the time was the leading try scorer in the Rugby Football League with 14 tries, including one at Wembley. He didn't play again in the season and he was sorely missed as the left-wing partnership of Senior and Crowther had set opposition defences a real challenge.

Darren Turner is checked by the St Helens defence as once again Eagles pip the Saints at the Don Valley. Eagles won 18-17 and started a run of five wins in six games, their only consistently successful period in Super League III. Gareth Stephens is the player coming up in support.

Mark Aston chalked up his 2,000th point for the club in the 1998 season. By the end of the campaign he had a tally of 2,013 points – comprised of 886 goals, 50 tries and 41 drop goals – since joining from Selby ARLFC in 1986. If Broadbent and Carr were the heart of the Eagles' engine room, then Aston was the tactical brains that gave direction to Eagles' attacking play and marshalled its defensive systems.

Eagles Alliance team won their division in August 1998 and are shown here celebrating with the trophy. In the centre is 'AJ' Okiwe, who first played for Eagles in 1991 after making quite a name for himself in American Football. On the extreme left is Arnold Hema, the Kiwi who played for the Eagles in their very first season and returned over a decade later to give experience to the Alliance team. From left to right: Arnold Hema, Wayne Flynn, Chris Molyneux, Ben Cooper, John Howitt, Dale Cardoza, 'AJ' Okiwe, Andy Richardson, Darren Summerill (with trophy), Rob North, Pete Rousso, Neil Law. Law had scored 33 tries during the season for the Alliance team and was loaned to Wakefield Trinity for the 1999 Super League season.

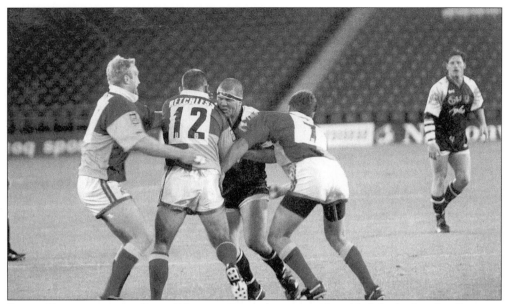

Darren Shaw in action at Bramall Lane in September against his old club, the London Broncos. A drop goal in the last minute gained London a narrow 19-18 win after a superbly contested game. Darren had been signed at the start of the season to replace Danny McAllister, who had unexpectedly stayed in Australia after returning for the winter. Shaw had had three seasons with London but came to Eagles from the Canberra Raiders, for whom he played in the 1997 season. Through the parent rule he qualified for Scotland and was their longest running international with 8 caps. In 1999 he was chosen to replace Broadbent as captain.

Doncaster Toll Bar ARLFC celebrate winning a junior rally at the Don Valley Stadium. Encouraging schools and junior amateur clubs was always a high priority for Eagles and in the 1998/99 season fifty-four teams from twenty-one secondary schools in the area participated in four leagues from under-13 to under-16 age levels.

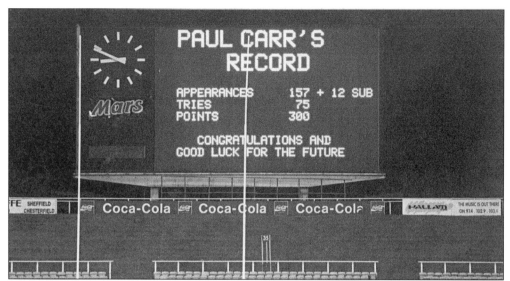

It was the end of the road for Paul Carr, the popular Aussie with the blockbuster tackle and the explosive burst through the opponents' line. He retired after the Warrington match in September and the scoreboard recorded his tremendous contribution to the Eagles since he joined the club in 1992. Along with Powell, Aston and Broadbent, he was one of four most significant players in the short history of the Sheffield club. He also dug up some Scottish ancestors and played one international game for Scotland to complete his record in British football.

Paul Broadbent addresses the crowd at the end of what had been an inconsistent season. The glory of the Cup Final win had not been sustained in Super league and the final tally of P23 W8 L13 D2, with a final position of eighth was something of an anti-climax. This was to be Paul Broadbent's last season with the club after 326 games for the Eagles since he joined from Lock Lane ARLFC in Castleford in 1987. He had become the established Great Britain prop forward with 8 Great Britain and 5 England caps to his credit. His departure to Halifax Blue Sox before the 1999 season was a considerable loss to the club.

Eagles line-up for the 1999 season. From left to right, back row: Janet Hornbuckle (doctor), Stephens, Sovatabua, Sodje, Richardson, Lovell, Powell, Windas, Pearson, Cardoza, Dean Mitchell (kit manager). Middle row: Steve Deakin (assistant coach), Simon Worsnop (conditioner), Wilkes, Molyneux, Turner, Baldwin, Anderson, Doyle, Molloy, Vassilakopoulos, Jackson, Ralph Rimmer (chief executive), Alan Tomlinson (physiotherapist). Front row: Crowther, Senior, Aston, John Kear (head coach), Shaw (captain), LG representative, Tim Adams (chairman), Hardy, Laughton, Lawless.

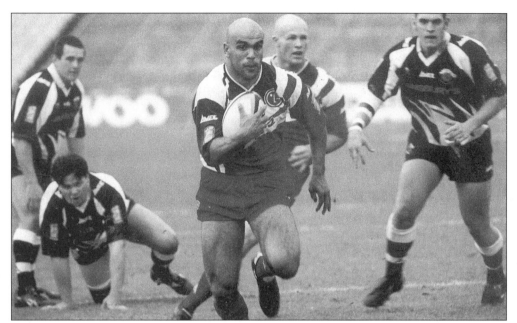

Jeff Hardy makes a break to score in Eagles' 22-12 win over Wakefield at Don Valley in April 1999. Jeff had returned to the Eagles after playing most of the decade with St George in Sydney. He played in three Grand Finals for the Dragons and was a welcome addition to Eagles' ranks after the departure of Paul Carr. Jeff had played for the Eagles as a young unknown in their first season in the top division in 1989/90 and he had scored twice in the great victory over Widnes at Bramall Lane. Eagles that year had had no ground of their own. Now Jeff returned in 1999 to Don Valley and Super League and commented that 'Things seemed to have moved on a bit over here'.

Eagles fans meet at a pre-season get together with the club officials and the players. This function was now a regular feature of the weeks immediately before the start of the campaign. However, in 1999 it was a particularly large, enthusiastic and expectant gathering that met in the Don Valley Stadium function room to hear Tim Adams, John Kear and the new captain Darren Shaw. Unfortunately, 1999 didn't prove to be a vintage year for the Sheffield team. After the season ended the club was merged with the Huddersfield Giants and its fifteen year history as an independent club in South Yorkshire came to an end.

Bright Sodje returns to the changing room, whilst Dale Cardoza continues to sign autographs for young fans after a disappointing start to the season. Eagles lost to London Broncos 20-26 after squandering a 20-8 lead with twenty minutes to go. Mike Turner wards off the rain in the background. Mike Turner was Eagles marketing manager for four years and did a great deal to give the club a more professional image as well as first class pre-match entertainment routines. He was one of the key men in the Eagles front office during the Super League years.

Billed as 'The Eagles' biggest ever signing', Mike Turner secured the 20ft inflatable player to add to the publicity for the club. Despite this monster signing, Eagles ended what turned out to be their final season in tenth place in the Super League with ten wins and one draw.

Six

The Greatest Day

2 May 1998

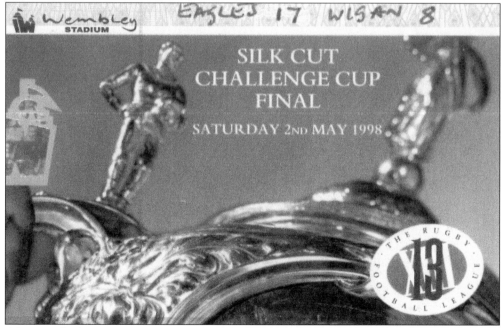

After nearly fourteen years in existence, Eagles won their way through to the 1998 Rugby League Challenge Cup final. Their opponents were Wigan, who had dominated the competition in recent years with eight consecutive wins beginning in 1988, but who had not been to Wembley since 1995. They were expected to regain the trophy by a considerable margin. Most people felt Eagles were only there to make up the numbers, but John Kear and the team had other ideas. They produced one of the greatest upsets, not just of Rugby League history, but of any major British sporting trophy in the last decade of the century.

Before the final, Eagles produced a T-shirt showing the four victories that had won them their place at Wembley. After the 17-8 win over Wigan, the T-shirt was amended and worn proudly by Eagles fans. Here it is modelled by Samantha Carr of Yewlands School.

Keith Senior struggles to break the Castleford defence in the quarter-final at Wheldon road. He had quite a match, scoring two tries in a thrilling 32-22 victory over the Tigers and also flooring B.J. Mather with one of the best executed uppercuts ever seen on BBC TV's *Grandstand*. This gained him a four-match ban and he had to sit out the semi-final against Salford. Doyle (left) and Sovatabua (right) are the Eagles observing the tackle.

The try that took Eagles to Wembley – Dale Laughton stretches out to score after a diagonal run behind the play-the-ball caught the Salford defence unprepared in the semi-final at Headingley. At 18-10 down in the second half, Eagles appeared to be going out of the Cup. Then Aston scored an opportunist try and three minutes later Laughton steamrollered over to ensure victory.

Paul Broadbent, presumably with tears of joy, being congratulated by a young supporter. Eagles had not played particularly well and Salford had been the better team for most of the match. However, the last fifteen minutes changed the course of the game and Eagles history.

Eagles were now the centre of much media attention as they prepared for the final. John Kear allowed press conferences and photo shoots until the final week and then the team went into seclusion to concentrate on the game and avoid any distractions as they planned their campaign. The most famous publicity stunt that captured the imagination of the nation's tabloid press was an adaptation of the theme of the film *The Full Monty*. The venue was Shiregreen Working Men's Club, which had been used for the final scene in the film itself. *Above*: The players preparing for the 'ordeal'. *Below*: The final product complete with strategically placed footballs.

Eagles fans met on Wembley Way and marched en-masse for the final two hundred yards to the stadium. Many had made the journey from Sheffield and they were delighted to find that all the neutral spectators at Wembley were Eagles supporters for the day.

Kath Owen (left) and her drum squad, suitably decked out for the occasion, led the march of Eagles fans up Wembley Way and into the stadium. At this point supporters felt delighted just to be in a final – however, the day was about to get even better.

Eagles and Wigan line up for the presentations with the band of the Prince of Wales' Own Regiment of Yorkshire in the middle of the pitch. Wigan had walked out full of confidence whilst Eagles had looked totally determined. Determination would carry the day.

One final hug before the battle. The preparation and the planning for this moment had been meticulous. John Kear's carefully plotted game plan was about to be unleashed on an unsuspecting Wigan.

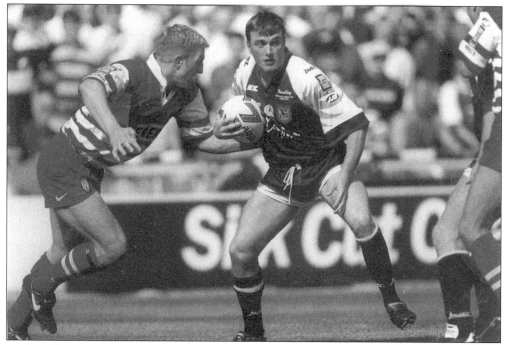

Nick Pinkney seeks a way through the Wigan defence as Dennis Betts moves to close him down. Shortly afterwards, Pinkney scored by plucking a high cross-field kick out of the air and crashing down for the first try after 4 minutes of play.

Matt Crowther makes a break supported by Doyle, with Haughton and Farrell left behind. Crowther scored the second try in the corner, to give Eagles an 11-2 half-time lead.

Nick Pinkney leaps onto the crowd of Eagles players congratulating Darren Turner on scoring Eagles' third and decisive try. Kris Radlinski (left) and Anthony Farrell (right), like many thousands at the ground and even more watching TV, just can't believe it.

The Wembley scoreboard records the final result. Eagles had achieved a 17-8 victory and dumbfounded every Rugby League pundit who ever drew breath. Old timers recalled that you had to go back to the 1930s to find such an unexpected result. However, Eagles were a Super League team with the vast majority of their players having some international experience. They should never have been written off by the public and the media, who now showed their delight with the plaudits they gave the Sheffield club. It was a very good day for Rugby League.

Paul Broadbent lifts the Rugby League Challenge Cup and salutes the crowd. Tim Adams, the chairman, with his arms outstretched mirrors the delight of the players. To the left of Broadbent are Aston, Pinkney, Laughton, Lawless, Wood, Senior and Crowther.

Darren Shaw, Martin Wood and Michael Jackson show their delight as they follow the parade of the cup around the stadium. Many thousands of Wigan supporters stayed to applaud the new Cup winners. This was a big gesture from the fans of a very big club.

Mark Aston was joined on the pitch by his son Cory. Mark, who kicked two conversions and one drop goal, was named the Lance Todd Trophy winner. The trophy goes to the player adjudged the Man of the Match by the Rugby League press. The trophy was a fitting reward, not just for his performance in the Cup Final, but for his key tactical role in the Eagles sides over the years. By winning this award Aston joined the game's immortals, whose names are inscribed on the plinth. Dave Watson was a close second choice for the trophy.

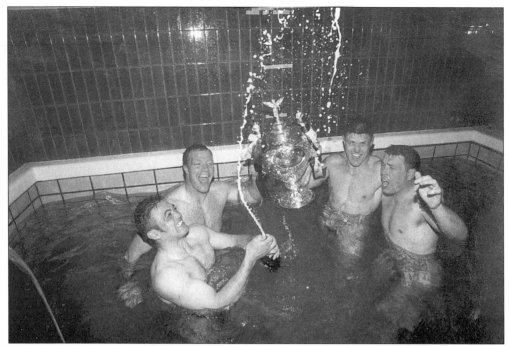

Eagles players continue the celebration in the plunge bath as Whetu Taewa uncorks the champagne, whilst Broadbent and Carr hold onto the Cup and Aston leads the singing.

Paul Broadbent and John Kear field questions at the official press conference. John Kear had told his team at the beginning of the season that they could win the Challenge Cup. He had carefully analysed the Wigan game plan and discovered weaknesses before directing his offensive tactics to exploit them. Kear had built a self-belief in his players which was particularly manifest in their unrelenting aggressive tackling. This placed a stranglehold on their opponents from which they never escaped during the 80 minutes of play.

Eagles players parade the Cup through Sheffield in an open topped bus on their way to a reception at the Town Hall. They had a week to celebrate before the next game. Ironically it was against Wigan at the Don Valley and the Warriors took their revenge in some style to win 36-6. It took the team some time to settle down after Wembley. During the rest of May they only won one league game out of five played.

John Kear, acknowledged by all as the architect of the Cup victory, holds the Challenge Cup aloft in Fargate just before the team enters the Town Hall for a civic reception. The Eagles had finally landed.